S0-ATV-327

WILLIAM BULMER
AND THE
SHAKSPEARE PRESS

WILLIAM BULMER
Adapted by John DePol

WILLIAM BULMER
AND THE
SHAKSPEARE PRESS

A Biography of William Bulmer
from *A Dictionary of Printers and Printing*
by C. H. Timperley, London, 1839

with an Introductory Note

ON THE BULMER-MARTIN TYPES
by LAURANCE B. SIEGFRIED
Syracuse University

Original Wood Engravings
by JOHN DE POL

Published by
SYRACUSE UNIVERSITY PRESS
In Observance of the Bicentennial of the
Birth of William Bulmer, 1757-1957

Library of Congress Catalog Card Number 57–14801

© 1957 SYRACUSE UNIVERSITY PRESS

Designed by Harvey Satenstein

Manufactured in the United States of America
by Book Craftsmen Associates, Inc., New York

A Note on the Bulmer-Martin Types

By LAURANCE B. SIEGFRIED

Professor of Graphic Arts in the
School of Journalism at Syracuse University

IT WAS GEORGE NICOL, bookseller to His Majesty King George III and later an associate of Bulmer's in W. Bulmer and Company and the Shakspeare Press, who "engaged the skilful talents of Mr. William Martin, of Birmingham, in cutting sets of types, after approved models, in imitation of the sharp and fine letter used by the French and Italian printers."

The quotation is from the Bulmer biography that follows and is somewhat qualified by the footnote

1

(note 2, see page 29), which states rather baldly: "His [Martin's] Roman and Italic types were decided imitations of Baskerville's."

Oddly enough, these are the only references to Martin's work in the biography. For some reason known only to himself, the biographer, in quoting from Bulmer's advertisement of the *Poems of Goldsmith and Parnell* (page 19), chose to omit Bulmer's mention of Martin, which reads in part: "The whole of the Types, with which this work has been printed, are executed by Mr. William Martin . . . a very ingenious young artist . . . who is at this time forming a Foundry, by which he will shortly be enabled to offer to the world a Specimen of Types, that will in a very eminent degree unite utility, elegance, and beauty." The omission is the less understandable in view of the fact that the biographer does quote Bulmer's statement that "The present volume [the *Poems*] . . . [is] particularly meant to combine the various beauties of Printing, Type-founding, Engraving, and Paper-making; as well with a view to ascertain the near approach to perfection which those arts have attained in this country, as to invite a fair competition with the best Typographical Productions of other nations. . . . Much pains have been bestowed on the present publication, to render it a complete Specimen of the Arts of Type and Block-Printing." Certainly Bulmer showed no disposition to minimize the importance of the part that Martin had played in the making of this volume.

William Martin, as the note mentioned above goes on to state, was the brother of Robert Martin, whom it describes as "the apprentice of Baskerville." But Robert Martin was much more than that; a journeyman with Baskerville for ten years, he later became his foreman and was the man whom Baskerville made his "agent" and to whom he turned over the "use of his whole printing apparatus" at a time when he had become disillusioned with printing and publishing—his books were not financially successful—and was trying to sell his types. (Baskerville later resumed control.) What the professional relationships of the brothers may have been is uncertain, but it would seem that William Martin learned his trade in the Baskerville foundry and practiced it there before coming to Nicol in London as a punch-cutter. It is hardly surprising, therefore, that he should have followed in Baskerville's typographic footsteps when he set up on his own as a type founder.

As for the "imitation of the sharp and fine letter used by the French and Italian printers"—which, for practical purposes, meant Didot and Bodoni— this came about partly through Bulmer's desire to provide a type which should match the wood engravings of his lifelong friend, Thomas Bewick, in color and brilliance; partly, as is implied in the advertisement, through the ambition of Bulmer and his associates in the Shakspeare Press to produce in England books which should equal if not excel the best work of the French and Italians, in particular the work of one Giambattista Bodoni of Parma. It is possible that Baskerville's types would have served Bulmer's purpose, but these by then had been sold, mostly in France, and were no longer available.

"Martin's types, both roman and italic," says Updike, in summary, "were cut to imitate Baskerville's, but with certain fortunate individualities. A more 'modern' quality had crept into these fonts, but they were very splendid of their kind."*

It was these types of William Martin's, used in the Boydell edition of Shakspeare, the *Poems of Goldsmith and Parnell*, and other books printed by

* D. B. Updike, *Printing Types: Their History, Forms, and Use,* Second Edition (Cambridge: Harvard University Press, 1937), Vol. II, p. 123.

Bulmer between 1792 and about 1820, which were recut in 1923 by the late Morris Benton of American Type Founders Company, and which Benton named after Bulmer.* More recently they were cut for machine composition by the Monotype Company, which also cut the larger sizes for display. In both the A.T.F. and Monotype versions, the Martin originals were faithfully followed

Perhaps the best way of gauging the quality of these Bulmer-Martin types and of the "fortunate individualities" which Martin infused into them is to compare them in certain details of design with Caslon, as representing the best of the pre-Baskerville Dutch-English oldstyles, and with Bodoni (in its accepted present-day version) as representing the post-Baskerville "moderns."

Caslon 471	Bulmer	Bodoni
h m	h m	h m
q p	q p	q p

Caslon, of course, shows the typical oldstyle characteristics—the bracketed serifs, the gradual

* From the "Advertisement" in the brochure showing the Bulmer Roman and Italic, published by American Type Founders Company.

swell or taper of the curves, the relatively less degree of contrast in weight between thick and thin elements—as against the thin, flat, horizontal serifs, the abrupt break from thin to thick in the curves, and the sharply contrasting stems and hairlines of the Bodoni. One would hardly say of the Bulmer that it "combines the best features of each," though in design it obviously lies between the two, but to this eye at least, there is a grace, a refinement, one could almost say an aristocratic quality about the Bulmer that is not evident in either of the others. Notice, for instance, the way the curves take off from the stems in the h and m, the careful modeling and careful placing of the weight of the curves in the loops of the p and q. One has the feeling that the Bulmer characters are the most painstakingly drawn, the best lettered, so to speak, of the three. By comparison, the Caslon is more workmanlike, sturdier, more definitely English (or do we only imagine this?); the Bodoni more assertive, more mechanical in a T-square-and-triangle sort of way, and—perhaps because of its excessive use in advertising these past many years—more commercial.

These qualities of the Bulmer are not necessarily assets as regards its readability when composed in mass—i.e., in book pages, in magazine pages and columns, and in large blocks of type in advertising. Not only Caslon but certain transitional faces, notably Baskerville and Caledonia, are slightly wider, letter for letter, and have a roundness, an openness of design, and a consequent "flow" which gives them probably greater legibility as body types and contributes to ease and speed of reading, particularly in the relatively wide measures in which most book pages are set. Bulmer, by contrast, is a lean face. Because of this, and because of its horizontal bottom serifs, it requires careful spacing and ample, almost Bodoniesque leading to be at its best. It is not a type to be used on any and every job, not a universal or all-purpose type, but rather an occasional, even a special-occasions face.

As against this, the Bulmer, being slightly heavier and more "contrasty," has more color than Caslon or Baskerville or Caledonia—Janson, among the oldstyles, probably approaches it closest in this respect—and, as a result, retains its color well on coated or calendered papers where many oldstyles and some of the lighter transitionals go gray and lose their character. Thanks to this color and to the careful modeling of the letters, it also gives a more interesting texture to a page—a quality more apparent to the professional than to the layman, who is only subconsciously aware of such things, if at all. Even so fine a face as Garamond, when printed in pages or columns on coated stock, has a way of presenting itself visually as an even-toned gray wash. And, given a "good black printing ink" (such as Bulmer first obtained through Robert Martin and later made for himself) and the spacing and leading it needs, the Bulmer fairly sparkles on a good antique. At the other end of the typographic scale, it is free from the stiffness, the mechanical quality, the eye-retarding verticality (if there is such a word!) of both the "regular" Bodoni and the lighter Bodoni Book—qualities which tend to tire the eye and cause the type to become monotonous and fatiguing when read for any considerable length of time. As to whether it fulfills the Paul Beaujon dictum that "type should be invisible"—i.e., that it should not intrude itself between author and reader, that the reader should never be conscious of it *as* type— well, does it or does it not do so in this book? *

There is not space here to show complete alphabets of the Bulmer in comparison with Caslon and

* The colophon, which appears at the back, lists the manufacturing specifications for this book.

Bodoni, and the only Baskerville available in sizes large enough for effective comparison is the Stephenson Blake-A.T.F. version, which, as the late Bruce Rogers once observed to the writer, is not a Baskerville but a Fry. However, alphabets of the roman and italic, both capitals and lowercase, are shown; and here again one sees the effective blending of Baskerville with Didot-Bodoni and of old-style with modern. Notice, in the roman lowercase, the bottom serifs, which resemble the flat serifs of the Bodoni but suggest bracketing if they are not actually bracketed; the top serifs of the ascending letters, which are slanted but not nearly so much so as in Caslon, for instance; the slanted top of the t, which is by Baskerville out of Caslon, so to speak— all this as against the generally "modern" feel of the letters. Except possibly for the retracting g with its round upper loop, the letters are free from any idiosyncrasies.

Again with possibly two exceptions—the rather sprightly Q and the low-waisted Y, both of which are modified Baskerville—the capitals (roman) show the same freedom from affectation, from any conscious striving for effect. They are well-mannered letters, beautiful, graceful, dignified, but their

9

A B C D E F G H I J K L M

N O P Q R S T U V W X Y Z

a b c d e f g h i j k l m n o p q r s t

u v w x y z . , - ' ' : ; ! ? fi fl ff ffi ffl

$ 1 2 3 4 5 6 7 8 9 0

A B C D E F G H I J K L M

N O P Q R S T U V W X Y Z

a b c d e f g h i j k l m n o p q r s t

u v w x y z . , - ' ' : ; ! ? fi fl ff ffi ffl

$ 1 2 3 4 5 6 7 8 9 0

18 POINT BULMER 497, ROMAN & ITALIC

manners are an integral part of them, not something assumed for an occasion. Like the lowercase, they have a definitely transitional quality, a combination of oldstyle and modern characteristics, and this quality makes the Bulmer one of the most adaptable of display faces—a face that can be used to excellent advantage with body matter set in any of the transitional types and in almost any oldstyle or modern. It has long been recognized as such by book designers, as has been evidenced in the "Fifty Books of the Year" exhibitions of the American Institute of Graphic Arts, and, from present indications, is coming more and more into its own in advertising and commercial printing as an alternative for the more emphatic and much overworked Bodoni and for the starkness of the sans serifs—and, it might be added (or hoped!), for the overweight, steatopygic square serifs that are such favorites currently among agency art directors. As a body type it has made less progress, mainly for the reason that it has been available only of late years on the machine.

The italic is closer than the roman to its Baskerville prototype and, possibly for that reason, is less successful. The lowercase is somewhat compressed, though less so than Baskerville's, and has a way of going feminine, sometimes almost to the point of effeminacy—a quality of which more advantage might be taken by advertisers selling to the ladies. There is a self-consciousness about the italic, an effect of prettiness, that is not present in the roman. One feels, too, that Martin might have done better, in his italic capitals, to break away from Baskerville in the swash-like character of the K, N, T, and Y —either that or provide both plain and swash versions of these letters. Possibly a larger admixture of Didot-Bodoni might have been of advantage here.

In spite of this weakness, however, one has the feeling that these Bulmer-Martin types are coming in on a rising typographic tide—subject, of course, to whatever may be the effects of further and as yet unforeseeable developments in phototypesetting, which so far has shown a disposition to adhere to historic types rather than attempt to evolve new forms of its own. It would seem to be something more than coincidence, something more than the mere fact of availability on the machines, that has led book and magazine and, yes, even advertising designers in recent years to the wider and wider use of transitional types—types like Baskerville, Caledonia, Monotype's Bell, Linotype's recent

Monticello, possibly even the Times Roman, which to the writer has more the "feel" of a transitional than of any other classification. This has been evident in the annual catalogues of the "Fifty Books of the Year" exhibitions; it has been evident in the surprisingly extensive recent comeback of Century and its derivatives, long considered typographic old hat, in newspaper and magazine advertising; it has been evident in such phenomena as the recent switch of the *Saturday Evening Post* to its Baskerville-cum-Times-Roman combination (Why, one wonders parenthetically, does it shift from Baskerville to Times Roman in its continuations?) and the wide-spread use of transitionals in trade, association, technical, and house publications, as well as in commercial printing. Whatever the reason, we Americans seem to *like* these transitionals. And we seem to be acquiring more and more of a liking for Bulmer and its "fortunate individualities."

William Caslon used Dutch oldstyles as his models in cutting his roman type (the Caslon Old Face). William Martin took his cue from Baskerville on the one hand and, possibly at Bulmer's instigation, certainly with his complete support and approval, from the Didot-Bodoni "modern" form of letter on the other. Similarly, in our own time, Bruce Rogers (as he has told) made letter-by-letter tracings from photographic enlargements of Nicolas Jenson's roman and used them as the starting point for his Centaur type. And it was from detailed study of the various forms of Scotch Roman, including the now forgotten Wayside, that Dwiggins (as he also has told, with illustrations) evolved his Caledonia.

Who is to say, with men like these, where imitation stops and creation and artistry begin?

WILLIAM BULMER
C. H. TIMPERLEY*

1830, *Sept.* 9. *Died*, WILLIAM BULMER, printer, whose name is associated with all that is correct and beautiful in typography. By him the art was matured, and brought to its present high state of perfection.

This celebrated typographer was a native of Newcastle-upon-Tyne, where he was apprenticed to Mr. Thompson, in the Burnt House-entry, St. Nicholas's Churchyard, from whom he received the first rudiments of his art. During his apprenticeship he formed a friendship with Thomas Bewick,

* From *A Dictionary of Printers and Printing* (London, 1839), 2 vols.

the celebrated engraver on wood, which lasted with great cordiality throughout life. It was their practice, whilst youths, to visit together every morning, a farm-house at Elswick, a small village about two miles from Newcastle, and indulge in Goody Coxen's hot rye-cake and buttermilk, who used to prepare these dainties for such of the Newcastle youths who were inclined to enjoy an early morning walk before the business of the day commenced. During the period of the joint apprenticeships of these young aspirants for fame, Bulmer invariably took off the first impressions of Bewick's blocks, at his master's printing-office, at Newcastle, where Bulmer printed the engraving of the Huntsman and Old Hound, which obtained for Bewick the premium from the society of arts, in London. Mr. Bulmer afterwards suggested to his friend Bewick an improvement, of which he availed himself, of lowering the surfaces of the blocks where the distance or lighter parts of the engraving were to be shown to perfection.

When Mr. Bulmer first went to London, his services were engaged by Mr. John Bell, who was then publishing his beautiful miniature editions of the poets, Shakspeare, &c. About 1787, an accidental circumstance introduced Mr. Bulmer to the late

George Nicol, esq.[1] bookseller to king George III. who was then considering the best method of carrying into effect the projected magnificent national edition of Shakspeare, which he had suggested to Messrs. Boydell, ornamented with designs by the first artists of the country. Mr. Nicol had previously engaged the skilful talents of Mr. William Martin,[2] of Birmingham, in cutting sets of types, after approved models, in imitation of the sharp and fine letter used by the French and Italian printers; which Mr. Nicol for a length of time caused to be carried on in his own house. Premises were then engaged in Cleveland-row, St. James's, and the "Shakspeare press" was established under the firm of "W. Bulmer and Co." This establishment soon evinced how judicious a choice Mr. Nicol had made in Mr. Bulmer to raise the reputation of his favourite project.

"This magnificent edition (says Dr. Dibdin) which is worthy of the unrivalled compositions of our great dramatic bard, will remain as long as those compositions shall be admired, an honourable testimony of the taste and skill of the individuals who planned and conducted it to its completion.[3] The text was revised by G. Steevens and Isaac Reed. Mr. Bulmer possessed the proof sheets of the whole work, on which are many curious remarks by Stee-vens, not always of the most courteous description; also some original sonnets, a scene for a burlesque tragedy, some graphic sketches, &c."

"The establishment of the Shakspeare press (con-tinues Dr. Dibdin) was unquestionably an honour both to the founders in particular, and to the pub-lic at large. Our greatest poet, our greatest painter, and two of our most respectable publishers and printers, were all embarked in one common white-hot crucible; from which issued so pure and bril-liant a flame or fusion that it gladdened all eyes and hearts, and threw a new and revivifying lustre on the threefold arts of painting, engraving, and print-ing. The nation appeared to be not less struck than astonished; and our venerable monarch George III. felt anxious not only to give such a magnificent es-tablishment every degree of royal support, but, in-fected with the matrix and puncheon mania, he had even contemplated the creation of a royal printing-office within the walls of his own palace!" One of his majesty's principal hopes and wishes was, for his own country to rival the celebrity of Parma in the productions of Bodoni; and Dr. Dibdin pleas-antly alludes to what he calls the Bodoni Hum,—

of "his majesty being completely and joyfully *taken in*, by bestowing upon the efforts of Mr. Bulmer's press, that eulogy which he had supposed was due exclusively to Bodoni's."

The first number of the *Shakspeare* appeared in January, 1794; and at once established Mr. Bulmer's fame as the first practical printer of the day. Dr. Dibdin has given (*Bibliographical Decameron*, ii. 384–395) a curious and copious list of the "books printed at the Shakspeare press," with judicious remarks, to which we must refer our readers, noticing only such as are the most eminent in execution. Next to the *Shakspeare*, perhaps the edition of the *Poetical Works of John Milton*, in 3 vols. folio, 1793–1797, is the finest production of Mr. Bulmer's press. Dr. Dibdin seems to prefer this work even to the *Shakspeare* itself.

In 1795, Mr. Bulmer printed a beautiful edition in 4to. of the *Poems of Goldsmith and Parnell*, one copy on white satin, and three on vellum. The volume is dedicated to the founders of the Shakspeare printing-office, Messrs. Boydells and Nicol. "The present volume," says Mr. Bulmer, in his advertisement, "in addition to the *Shakspeare*, the *Milton*, and many other valuable works of elegance, which have already been given to the world through the medium of the Shakspeare press, are [is] particularly meant to combine the various beauties of printing, type-founding, engraving, and paper making; as well with a view to ascertain the near approach to perfection which those arts have attained to this country, as to invite a fair competition with the best typographical productions of other nations. How far the different artists who have contributed their exertions to this great object, have succeeded in the attempt, the public will now be fully able to judge. Much pains have been bestowed on the present publication to render it a complete specimen of the arts of type and block-printing. The ornaments are all engraved on blocks of wood, by my earliest acquaintances, Messrs. Bewicks, of Newcastle-upon-Tyne and London, after designs from the most interesting passages of the poems they embellish. They have been executed with great care, and I may venture to say, without being supposed to be influenced by ancient friendship, that they form the most extraordinary effort of the art of engraving upon wood, that ever was produced in any age, or any country. Indeed, it seems almost impossible that such delicate effects could be obtained from blocks of wood.[4]

Of the paper it is only necessary to say, that it comes from the manufactory of Mr. Whatman." Besides the wood-cuts, the work was embellished with eight very superior vignettes.—The biographical sketches of Goldsmith and Parnell, prefixed to the work, were by Isaac Reed.—This volume was highly appreciated by the public; two editions of it, in 4to. were sold, and they produced a profit to the ingenious printer, after payment of all expenses, of £1,500.

Stimulated by the great success of the work, Mr. Bulmer, in 1796, was induced to prepare an embellished quarto edition of *Somerville's Chase*. Three copies were printed on vellum. It is thus dedicated,

"To the Patrons of fine Printing:"

"When the exertions of an individual to improve his profession are crowned with success, it is certainly the highest gratification his feelings can experience. The very distinguished approbation that attended the publication of Goldsmith's *Traveller, Deserted Village*, and Parnell's *Hermit*, which was last year offered to the public, as a specimen of the improved state of typography in this country, demands my warmest acknowledgments; and is no less satisfactory to the different artists who contributed their efforts towards the completion of the work. The *Chase*, by Somerville, is now given as a companion to *Goldsmith*; and it is almost superfluous to observe, that the subjects which ornament the present volume, being entirely composed of landscape scenery, and animals, are adapted, above all others, to display the beauties of wood-engraving." In 1804, the above two works were reprinted in one octavo volume, by Mr. Bulmer, with the same embellishments, for Messrs. Cadell and Davies, who had purchased the blocks.

Museum Worsleyanum, 1798–1803, 2 vols. folio, English and Italian. Sir Richard Worsley[5] expended £27,000 on this work, which was never published.[6] *Portraits of the Sovereigns of the Turkish Empire*, with biographical sketches in French and English; large folio. By John Young, esq. This work was printed at the expense of the sultan Selim, and the whole impression was sent to the Ottoman court. *The Antiquities of the Arabs in Spain*, by Cavannah Murphy, 1816, large folio. This herculean folio rivals Denon's[7] *Egypt*, in nobleness of design, splendour of execution, and richness of material. *The History of the Arabs in Spain, &c.* 4to. 1816. This volume is a companion to the above. *The Typographical Antiquities of Great Britain*, by T. F. Dibdin.

Vols. ii., iii., and iv. The union of the red and black inks, the proportioned spaces, and the boldness and singularity of the cuts, render these books very beautiful of their kind. *Bibliotheca Spenceriana*, 4 vols.[8] This work, considering the bulk of the volumes, and the quantity of matter introduced, is perhaps the most brilliant bibliographical production in existence, on the score of mere typographical excellence. Only fifty-five copies were struck off upon large paper, in royal 4to., eight of which were reserved by earl Spencer for presents. Upon the completion of this work, carried on without intermission for nearly four years, the printer presented Dr. Dibdin with a richly-wrought silver cup, of an antique form.[9]

Of all the works executed at the Shakspeare press, the *Bibliographical Decameron*, three vols. 8vo. by T. F. Dibdin, is acknowledged to be the most eminently successful in the development of the skill and beauty attached to the art of printing. Never was such a variety of ornament—in the way of woodcuts and red and black ink—exhibited.[10] The quantity of matter, by way of note, is perhaps no where exceeded, in a performance which unites splendour of execution with curiosity of detail. The paper is also of the finest quality. We have not space to enumerate the private reprints of Mr. Bulmer for the Roxburghe club, the history of which will be found in Dibdin's *Bibliographical Decameron*, vol. iii., pp. 69–74.

One of the chief difficulties Mr. Bulmer had to contend with, was the providing of good black printing ink. That formerly used by printers was execrable. Baskerville had made his own ink, as well as type, about 1760, which enabled him to produce such fine work; and Mr. Robert Martin,[11] his apprentice, was still living when Mr. Bulmer began business. He first supplied Mr. Bulmer with fine lampblack, for his experiments in fine printing; but the difficulty of obtaining an adequate supply, induced Mr. Bulmer to erect an apparatus for the purpose of making his own ink, and he succeeded to the extent of his wishes in producing a very superior black. In the *Shakspeare*, which was nine years in hand, the same harmony of tint and richness of colour prevail, as if the ink had been all made at one time, and the last sheet inked by the same hand in the same hour as the first: this single work probably contains more pages than Bodoni ever printed. Much must have been owing to the aid of good and congenial quality in the paper, and insured in effect by the experience and skill which Mr. Bulmer was so competent to impart to his workmen;[12] and that a great deal must have depended on, and been effected by, the two last-named requisites, is very apparent, from his being able to produce the same effect in ink of another colour, namely red.

After continuing in business with the highest credit for about thirty years, Mr. Bulmer retired in 1819, with a well-earned fortune, to a genteel residence at Clapham Rise, and was succeeded at the Shakspeare press by his partner, Mr. William Nicol, the only son of his friend. Mr. Nicol, in his *Octoglot* folio edition of *Virgil*, edited by W. Sotheby, esq. has proved himself a most diligent and able successor. But whilst we have justly placed Mr. Bulmer in the first rank of his profession, let us not forget that he had equal claims to distinction among those whose memory is revered for their many private and domestic virtues. We may then truly say, that his art was deprived of its brightest ornament, and his friends had to lament the loss of one not easily surpassed in every moral excellence.

Mr. Bulmer was one of the oldest members of the honourable band of gentlemen pensioners, and of which William Gifford[13] was paymaster. It was the practice of Mr. Gifford, whenever an exchequer warrant was issued for the payment of the quarterly salaries of the gentlemen of the band, to inform its members, by a circular letter, that their salaries were in a course of payment; but on many of these occasions he was wont to depart from his usual routine, and indulge himself in a poetical notice to Mr. Bulmer. From a variety of these momentary effusions of the satirist, we select the following:[14]

An Admonitory Epistle to the Right Worthy Gentleman,
W. Bulmer, Gentleman Pensioner.

"O thou who safely claim'st the right to stand
Before thy king, with dreaded axe in hand,
My trustiest Bulmer! know upon my board
A mighty heap of *cash* (O golden word!)
Now lies for service done, the bounteous meed,
Haste then, in Wisdom's name, and hither speed:
For if the truth old poets sing or say,
Riches straight make them wings and fly away!"

To William Bulmer, esq. brother to Sir Fenwick Bulmer, knight.[15]

SEPT. 1821

"Dread Sir, whose blood, to knighthood near,
Is sixpence now an ounce more dear
   Than when my summons issued last;
With cap in hand, I beg to say,
That I have money to defray
   The service of the quarter past."

Mr. Bulmer died at Clapham Rise, on the 9th of September, in his 74th year, and his remains were interred on the 16th, at St. Clement Danes, Strand (in which parish his brother had long resided) attended to the grave by a numerous and respectable company of mourning friends. He left a widow; but had no children. The portrait which we present of Bulmer, is from one faithfully executed in lithography, in 1827, painted and drawn on stone by James Ramsay.

Notes to *William Bulmer*

1. George Nicol was many years bookseller to George III., and one who may be justly designated, as Dr. Campbell said of Thomas Davies, "not a bookseller, but a gentleman dealing in books." He was at first placed under his uncle, David Wilson, of the Strand; and was by him taken into partnership in 1773. Mr. Wilson dying at an advanced age in 1777, Mr. Nicol removed his business to Pall Mall. On Sept. 8, 1787, Mr. Nicol married the accomplished niece of the first alderman Boydell. It was suspected that he was a sleeping partner in the "Shakspeare Press;" and to which his son, Mr. William Nicol, succeeded, as the sole proprietor, on Mr. Bulmer's retiring, in 1819. Mr. Nicol was, in 1797, one of the executors of Mr. James Dodsley, the bookseller, of Pall Mall, who left him a legacy of £1,000. Mr. Nicol was a most agreeable companion; and, perhaps, no man ever enjoyed the pleasure of convivial society more than he did. He was a member of many of the literary clubs of his day; was the publisher of many valuable works; and enjoyed the friendly confidence of the duke of Roxburghe, duke of Grafton, and other eminent bibliopists. He died

at his house in Pall Mall, London, June 25, 1829, at the age of 88 years.

2. William Martin was brother of Robert Martin, the apprentice of Baskerville. He afterwards set up a foundry in Duke-street, St. James's. His Roman and Italic types were decided imitations of Baskerville's; but his Greeks and Orientals formed the most valuable part of his collection. His foundry, in 1817, was united to the Caslon. This ingenious letter-founder died in the summer of 1815, and was buried in St. James's church, Westminster.

3. Mr. Nicol's connexion with the Messrs. Boydell was productive of one of the largest literary speculations ever embarked in in this country. The well known Boydell edition of our immortal bard originated with Mr. Nicol, in a conversation that took place in the year 1797, as appears by a paper, written and printed by Mr. Nicol, giving an account of what he had done for the improvement of printing in this country. The fate of that national undertaking, the "Shakspeare Gallery," in Pall Mall, was unfortunate; it cost the proprietors above £100,000. It was adjoining to Mr. Nicol's house, and intended for the exhibition of the original paintings. The great object of the undertaking was to establish an English school of historical painting.

4. It is said that George III. entertained so great a doubt on the subject, that he ordered his book-

seller, Mr. Nicol, to procure the blocks from Mr. Bulmer for his inspection, that he might convince himself of the fact.

5. Sir Richard Worsley, bart. died in the isle of Wight, August 8, 1805, in the fifty-fourth year of his age.

6. £400 has been given for a copy at a book-sale.

7. Baron Denon, a celebrated traveller, died at Paris, April 28, 1825.

8. *Bibliotheca Spenceriana: or a descriptive catalogue of the books printed in the fifteenth century, and of many valuable first editions, in the library of George John earl Spencer.* By the rev. T. F. Dibdin, 3 vols. imp. 8vo. 1814.

The right hon. George John Spencer, earl Spencer, viscount Althorpe, K.G., F.R.S., F.S.A., &c. &c. was born Sept. 1, 1758, and in 1783 succeeded his father in his titles and princely fortune. It was the delight of this eminent nobleman to collect around him the most learned literary and scientific men of the age, and wherever his patronage could be of use in promoting and extending literary and scientific knowledge it was liberally and munificently given. In bibliographical acquirements earl Spencer was considered equal to any man of his time, and the noble library which he collected at Althorpe, Northamptonshire, ranks amongst the most perfect and valuable of its kind in Europe. Throughout his life he was the able defender of an enlightened and liberal policy—the friend and coadjutor of Fox and Grey. In private life lord Spencer was no less distinguished for private worth, than for public principle in the high and important offices which he had held in the state. He died at Althorpe, Nov. 10, 1834.

9. See *Bibliographical Decameron*, vol. ii. page 394.

10. If we are not dazzled by the exquisite typography, the paper, and the engravings of Dr. Dibdin's productions, we cannot be blind to the superficial acquirements of the author.—*Partington*. See the preface to the *Catalogue of Books and Tracts printed at the private press of George Allan, esq.* By John Trotter Brockett.

11. It has already been noticed, under the life of Baskerville (see page 733 *ante*), that he was weary of printing; and it appears, that after the publication of the folio bible, 1763, he at least declined to carry it on except through the medium of a confidential agent. This agent was Robert Martin, as appears by the following announcement: "Robert Martin has agreed with Mr. Baskerville for the use of his whole printing apparatus, with whom he has wrought as a journeyman for ten years past. He therefore offers his services to print at Birmingham, for gentlemen or booksellers, on the most moderate terms, who may depend on all possible care and ele-

gance in the execution. Samples, if necessary, may be seen, on sending a line to John Baskerville or Robert Martin."

12. One of the pressmen of this establishment was a well known and highly respected journeyman printer, named Daniel Grimshaw, a native of Lancashire; born in the year 1758, and in 1773, apprenticed to the late Mr. Ayres, printer and bookseller, at Warrington; an artist who was long considered the head of his profession in the north of England. At the expiration of his time, Mr. Grimshaw went to London, and found employment in the house of Mr. Bulmer, where the advantages he had derived in the country proved of such essential service as to render him competent to undertake the best works executed in that office, and often to receive from his employer marks of his respect for attention to his duty; so much so, that at one time Mr. Bulmer offered him an official situation, which he modestly declined. After several years' residence in London, Mr. Grimshaw returned to Manchester, where he was equally respected as a sober, industrious, and attentive workman, and looked upon as an honour to his profession. During the last twenty years of his life he enjoyed but a very indifferent state of health; and to the honour of the journeymen printers of Manchester be it said, that during the greater portion of that period, he was almost

supported by their praiseworthy benevolence. About eight years before his decease, his mental faculties became so much impaired that he was rendered wholly incapable of working. He died 17th March, 1838, at Warrington.

13. William Gifford, author of the *Baviad* and *Maviad*, translator of *Juvenal* and *Persius*, editor of the plays of *Massinger*, *Jonson*, and *Shirley*, also editor of the *Anti-jacobin* and *Quarterly Review*, was born at Ashburton, in Devonshire, in 1757, and from the low origin of a country shoe mender, by perseverance in the pursuit of knowledge and fortunate circumstances, became the first writer and satirist of the age. To his translation of *Juvenal* is prefixed a truly interesting account of himself. But while all must applaud the extraordinary talents with which he was endowed, it is a lamentable fact, that William Gifford, with determined hostility and persevering dislike, opposed the interests and hopes of the portion of society to which he himself originally belonged. He seems to have felt the necessity of vindicating his new position by contempt for his former associates; to have proved the sincerity of his apostacy from plebeianism by tenfold hostility to all but the aristocracy; and to have made use of his elevation only to trample upon those with whom he was formerly on a level. He died at London, Dec. 31, in his 71st year. In 1825, John Gibson Lock-

hart succeeded to the editorship of the *Quarterly Review*, under whom the work has advanced to a higher reputation than it ever before possessed, both as a political and literary journal.

14. See Nichols's *Illustrations*, vol. vi. pages 27–29.

15. Mr. Bulmer's elder brother, as the senior member of the band of gentlemen pensioners, was knighted on occasion of the coronation of George IV. He resided in the Strand, and died May 7, 1824, aged seventy-nine years.

Wood engravings
by John DePol

The entire book was set in Monotype Bulmer and printed by letterpress on Celluproof, manufactured especially for this edition by the Allied Paper Corporation. The covering material is Bancroft's Kennett.

Original wood engravings are by JOHN DEPOL.

Book design is by HARVEY SATENSTEIN.